every teen girl's little pink book

by Cathy Bartel

Harrison House
Tulsa, Oklahoma

Unless otherwise indicated, all Scripture quotations are taken from the *King James Version* of the Bible.

Scripture quotations marked NIV are taken from the *Holy Bible, New International Version*®. Copyright © 1973, 1978, 1984 by International Bible Society. Used by permission of Zondervan. All rights reserved.

Scripture quotations marked AMP are taken from the *Amplified® Bible*, copyright © 1954, 1958, 1962, 1964, 1965, 1987 by The Lockman Foundation. Used by permission. (www.Lockman.org).

Scripture quotations taken from the *New Life Version* (NLV), copyright © by Christian Literature International.

Scripture quotations marked NLT are taken from the *Holy Bible, New Living Translation*, copyright © 1996 by Tyndale Charitable Trust. Used by permission of Tyndale House Publishers.

Scripture quotations marked MSG are taken from *The Message*. Copyright © 1993, 1994, 1995, 1996, 2000, 2001, 2002 by Eugene H. Peterson. Used by permission of NavPress Publishing Group.

Scripture quotations marked NKJV are taken from the *New King James Version*. Copyright © 1982 by Thomas Nelson, Inc. Used by permission. All rights reserved.

10 09 08 07 06   10 9 8 7 6 5 4 3 2

every teen girl's little pink book
ISBN 13: 978-1-57794-792-9
ISBN 10: 1-57794-792-4
Copyright © 2006 by Cathy Bartel
P.O. Box 691923
Tulsa, Oklahoma 74179

Published by **Harrison House**, Inc.
P.O. Box 35035
Tulsa, Oklahoma 74153

Printed in the United States of America. All rights reserved under International Copyright Law. Contents and/or cover may not be reproduced in whole or in part in any form without the express written consent of the Publisher.

dedication

This book is dedicated to my dad and mom, Gerry and Donna Hunt. I love you with all of my heart and I am so honored to be your daughter. xoxoxo

I would also like to dedicate this book to Blake and Elaine Bartel. You are my parents by law (in-laws) but even more so by love. Thank you, dad and mom. I love you.

acknowledgments

To Blaine: Thank you for asking me to marry you! Thank you for being such a wonderful husband and father! I love being your wife and I love our life. xoxoxo

To Jeremy: Thank you for being a great teacher and telling me to just write from my heart. Speaking of hearts, bub, you have such a good and generous one. I love you so much and love being your mum.

To Dillon: Thank you for encouraging me and listening to my stories. I am honored to be the mom of such a kind and thoughtful young man. I love how you genuinely care about others and I sure do love you.

To Brock: Thank you for listening to my pink stories and coaching me. I admire how diligent you are in everything you do and I love how you enjoy life. I enjoy being your mom. I love you.

To my heavenly Father: Thank You for this opportunity to encourage Your daughters. I love You.

contents

introduction 9

delight 13

aspire 22

unashamed 29

generous 38

honor 45

thankful 53

encourage 61

relationships 69

a letter from Dad 77

a daughter's prayer 80

Dear friend,

Although you and I may not have ever met, I feel very honored to have this opportunity to remind you of something so amazing: *You are God's daughter!* Now, if you're unsure of that, I pray that this book will help you to know whom you belong to. God, your heavenly Father, created you with a heart that longs to be in a relationship with Him.

Think about this for a moment: God, the One who created the whole universe, formed you in your mother's womb and called you to be His daughter. How important does that make you feel? You are the daughter of the King of kings and Lord of lords! You could be called a princess! I know it makes me want to hold my head up so high, and at the same time bow down in humility!

One day when I was praying, the Lord reminded me that if I would make my relationship with Him the most important one—spending time with Him in prayer, studying His Word, and worshipping

Him—then He would help me do well in all the other things He has called me to do.

Now, take a look at this list of roles you may have as a young woman: daughter to your heavenly Father, daughter to your earthly parents, sister, granddaughter, niece, cousin, friend, best friend, student, teenager, babysitter, cheerleader, athlete, etc. As time goes on, you will gain new roles, such as employee, employer, aunt, girlfriend, fiancé, wife, daughter-in-law, sister-in-law, mother, mother-in-law, grandma, great-grandma. Oh my! As women, we wear a lot of hats.

Just remember: You don't have to wear all these hats at once. Thank goodness! I'm so thankful there are seasons in life, and the Lord prepares and equips us to take on all of these responsibilities as they come.

I am so thrilled for you to get to be a young woman in the times we are living in. He has called you for such a time as this. Trust your heavenly Father. He loved you so much that He gave His only Son, Jesus, so that if you believe in Him you will not perish but have everlasting life. You were bought with a great price! God gave His Son for you so you could be His daughter!

Have you ever seen the show *Trading Spaces*? Well, Jesus completely traded spaces with you—and not just for two days, but forever! He makes an eternal, forever, and always trade with you when you give your whole heart to Him. Some people call it The Great Exchange.

We give Him:	He gives us:
Our failures	His new beginnings
Our weaknesses	His strength
Our sadness	His joy
Our problems	His solutions
Our broken hearts	His comfort
Our pain	His healing
The impossible	"All things are possible"
Our dreams	His fulfillment
Our gifts and talents	His grace

I pray that this book will encourage you and help you to see how good God is and how precious you are to Him. I love you and want to see you grow more in love with God every day and be delighted to be His daughter!

Love,
Cathy

de-light

to take great pleasure to give keen enjoyment; to give joy or satisfaction to

Psalm 37:4 NIV says, "Delight yourself in the Lord and he will give you the desires of your heart." What do you think about that? I have to tell you, this Scripture is so dear to my heart! When I was a teenager I realized that if I would want to please the Lord in everything, He would not only give me the desires of my heart but would actually place His desires for me in my heart—and make them come true!

How amazing is that? Because you love God as your Father and because He loves you as His daughter, your desires and His desires for you become one desire! Remember: He has the absolute best plan for you.

You may be thinking, *How will I know it's God's desires I am following?* His Word and His will for you will agree. If you are delighting in the Lord, you'll be reading His Word. And if you're reading His Word, He will reveal His will to you.

Even though I haven't met you, I know you want to grow in your relationship with the Lord. Why else would you be reading this book? (By the way, I'd like to thank you. I'm very honored that you are sharing this time with me.)

As you grow in your relationship with God, you may wonder how else you can "delight yourself in the Lord."

Well, how do you take delight in your friends? You spend time with them. You talk with them, and you listen to them. Spending time with your heavenly Father is the best way to delight in Him, too. Here are a few ways you can spend time with Him:

 Read the Bible. The Bible contains love letters to you from God.

 Talk to Him. Listen to what God has to say to you, and tell Him how much you love Him.

 Spend time with others who know Him. Go to church and Bible studies, read books like this, and listen to teaching CDs.

Worship. Take time to tell God how much you appreciate all the good things He does for you.

Shortly after I asked Jesus to live in my heart, at around 14 years old, I was at church while an evangelist was speaking. For some reason, I looked over at his wife and thought, *I want to be a preacher's wife.* I admired her! Now, previous to that, the desire of my heart was to grow up and become a wife and a mother. Now I wanted so much to be a *preacher's* wife and a mother.

At that time, and throughout high school, I had a friend who was very annoying and would tease me to tears. I never would have imagined that he would become my husband. I had no idea if he would even have anything to do with becoming a Christian, let alone preaching the Gospel.

To make a long story short, he called me up about a year after we graduated and asked if I would like to be on a children's ministry team with him. He had been away at Bible school for a year and had learned a lot about ministering to kids with puppets and drama. My first thought was *I'll have to see this to believe it*. Well, to my surprise, he was serious—and the more I was around him, the more I literally fell in love with him. Here was a young man who loved God with all of his heart!

The desire the Lord had put in my heart several years before began to unfold right before my eyes. Blaine asked me to marry him, and for the last 25 years I have been so blessed to be at his side while he's preached to thousands of children, teenagers, and adults. Not only that, but for the last 21 years I've been busy fulfilling my dream of being a mom to three wonderful sons. I'm so thankful I delighted in the Lord and continue to do so! I know you will be thankful as you delight in the Lord, too!

Remember that God delights in you and is thinking of you right now.

> The Lord your God is with you…He will take great delight in you, He will quiet you with his love, He will rejoice over you with signing.
>
> Zephaniah 3:17 NIV

think pink

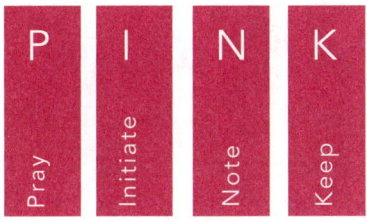

Lord, I thank You that as I delight myself in You, You give me the desires of my heart. Thank You for putting Your desires for me in my heart. Thank You for Your Word. As I study it, You write it on my heart. I hear Your voice; You are a good Father and a stranger's voice I do not follow.

de-light

You said in Your Word that You rejoice over me with singing. You calm me with Your love. You are my Savior and my Lord. I delight to do Your will, and I want to please You with all my heart. I look to Your Word because it is a lamp unto my feet and a light unto my path.

pink ponder

"To a father growing old, nothing is dearer than a daughter."

—Euripides[ii]

de-light

pink power

if God had a refrigerator

If God had a refrigerator,
your picture would be on it.

If He had a wallet, your photo
would be in it.

He sends you flowers every spring
and a sunrise every morning.

Whenever you want to talk,
He'll listen.

He can live anywhere in
the universe, and
He chose your heart.

What about the Christmas gift He sent you in Bethlehem, not to mention that Friday at Calvary?

Face it, friend. He's crazy about you.

—Author Unknown

as-pire *to seek to attain or accomplish a particular goal*

ascend, soar[iii]

What a wonderful thing to be able to say as a young woman, "Imitate me as I imitate Jesus"! Paul was able to say this (1 Cor. 11:1), and we should all be on our way to saying it, if we can't say it yet.

I believe we can admire others. It's nice to look up to people and think they're something special, but let's take it a step further and aspire to be like those people in our lives whom we admire. I'm not talking about people who look like they are successful but whose lives are falling apart behind closed doors. I want you to think about those people in your life who are tried and true. They are the real thing. Nobody's perfect, but it's good to admire the people in your life who genuinely show the love of God to others.

Because we're talking about God's daughters, I want you to think of older women you want to be like. (I know you can think of at least one.) It might be your very own mom, a big sister, an aunt, a teacher, a pastor's wife, or a friend. There are people in our lives who challenge us to grow up, to do better and try harder, to be more disciplined, to love more, to smile, to love ourselves, to help others, to be more like Jesus. Just being around them, we know they have spent time with the Lord. They share His joy and compassion. If you don't know someone like that, I pray right now for God to put a godly woman like that in your life. I believe that you'll know the blessing of this kind of relationship very soon, because it is so important.

It's also important that you be someone others look up to. Your example (good or bad) will speak louder than anything you say. You need to be that person whom others look up to when they are down. Be the girl at school, church, or even the mall who inspires some little girl to say to herself, "I want to be just like her." It will thrill your heart to hear someone say, "I've been watching you, and there is something you have that I don't. What is it?" Guess what? You are a witness of the love of Christ. You are an ambassador. You are God's daughter—a daughter of not just a king but of *the King of kings*.

Being a Christian is not always easy. You will sometimes have to make choices that are opposite of the average teenager's. However, may I remind you, you are not average! Every time you choose to obey God's Word (your Father's letters to you), He will give you strength to conquer temptations. Others will be watching you, longing for the stability, wisdom, and strength that you demonstrate as God's daughter.

Remember: Aspire to be like someone great, and be someone others aspire to be!

think pink

1 CORINTHIANS 11:1 AMP

Pattern yourselves after me [follow my example], as I imitate and follow Christ (the Messiah).

as-pire

pink ponder

You are daughters of God. If each one of you could only have a sure knowledge of this for yourself, you would have a sweet peace in your heart and confidence to meet any challenges life may bring.

Jayne B. Malin[iv]

pink power

7 questions to ask your parents in the next 7 days

Asking questions is a great way to learn and grow. When you ask others about yourself, you gain a perspective on areas of your life that you may have never realized. Here are 7 questions to ask your parents in the next 7 days. Write down their answers. Then look closely, and learn as you read each one.

 1. How can I be a better daughter?

 2. What do you see as my greatest strengths?

 3. What do you think are the weaknesses that I must work on?

 4. Which friends do you see as the best influences in my life?

as·pire

What kind of career could you see me getting into after I graduate?

 When do I make you most proud?

 What is the most important thing you've learned in life?

un-a-shamed

not ashamed

being without guilt, self-consciousness, or doubt

Psalm 3:2-4 brings so much comfort to me. I pray as you read it, you'll understand how much your heavenly Father wants for you to walk upright, knowing you are right with Him.

> Many are saying of me "There is no help for him in God." But You, O Lord, are a covering around me, my shining-greatness, and the One Who lifts my head. I was crying to the Lord with my voice. And He answered me from His holy mountain.
>
> *Psalm 3:2-4 NLV*

I can just see the Father right now, gently putting His hand under your chin and lifting your head up, looking you in the eyes and saying, "You're forgiven."

His Word says that if we confess our sins He is faithful and just to forgive us and make our lives clean. (1 John 1:9.)

Psalm 51:7 NLT says:

> Purify me from my sins, and I will be clean; wash me, and I will be whiter than snow.

I grew up in western Canada and spent a lot of time in the mountains. There is nothing like a fresh snowfall, when everything is completely covered in at least a foot of snow. It's so beautiful and sparkling clean. It just glistens.

When we've sinned (and we all know when we have), it's absolutely our responsibility as God's daughter to ask the Lord to forgive us, to receive His forgiveness, and in some cases to ask others to forgive us. When we do, we are just like that snow—clean and glowing.

> Come now, and let us reason together, saith the Lord: though your sins be as scarlet, they shall be as white as snow;

though they be red like crimson, they shall be as wool.

Isaiah 1:18

One time when I was about 16 and had just started driving, some of us were hanging out and talking in front of a friend's house. A boy from school pulled up, and we were all talking to him at his car. As he was leaving, he backed up to turn around and backed right into my car. Then he told me not to tell my dad and mom because he didn't have insurance. Because he was a senior football player and I was a little intimidated by him, I agreed to tell my parents that it must have happened in the school parking lot and that I didn't have a clue who did it.

I went home and proceeded to lie to my parents, but I felt sick. I couldn't sleep that night, and I was sick to my stomach the next day at school. I loved my parents, and I had been a Christian for a couple of years so I knew I had sinned. God's daughters don't lie.

I couldn't wait to get home from school that day to tell the truth. On my way, I pulled over in my

'66 red Chevy and prayed, "Lord, please forgive me for lying, and give me the courage and strength to tell my parents the truth...and don't let that boy beat me up." (He was a big boy—and not a very nice one.)

When I prayed, I knew I was on the right track but still had to obey God's Word and honor my parents by telling them the truth. I knew there would be consequences, but I also knew I was going to be able to hold my head up again. Doing the right thing and facing the punishment I would receive was so much better than walking around ashamed!

If I'd kept the lie going, what kind of a witness would that have been to the boy and all the other people who knew I was a Christian—including my own family, whom I was trying to reach?

Had I ever blown it just because I was afraid of a middle linebacker! I found out that day that no matter how much you think you've blown it with God, He is always faithful to His Word. The minute I told my parents the truth, the words "white as snow," "clean," "forgiven," and "right-standing" all became more real to me than ever—and I was relieved! I felt like a new girl.

I still hadn't faced that boy, but because I had done what was right, I wasn't afraid anymore. My parents forgave me, and the boy had to pay to fix my car. Thankfully, he didn't beat me up, but I did get a few dirty looks from him the rest of the school year!

Whenever you've been shown mercy, it can't stop there. The Lord wants you to hold your head up so you can help others hold their heads up, look into their eyes, and show them God's love, His truth, and His mercy. That's what it's all about.

God gave His Son, Jesus, who shed His blood so you and I can stand forgiven and unashamed with our head held high, so we can help heal a hurting world. I know you want to be that kind of young woman.

think pink

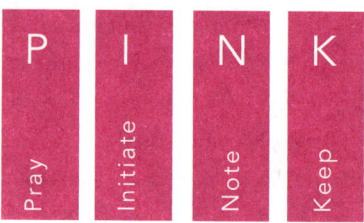

Lord, I just want to thank You for forgiving me of all my sins and washing me white as snow. I don't have to be ashamed, because You forgive me and are so patient with me. I love You!

pink ponder

Keep your thoughts right—for as you think, so you are. Thoughts are things; therefore, think only the things that will make the world better and you unashamed.

—Henry H. Buckley[vi]

pink power

3 things you must tell your parents

Communication is the key to victory in any kind of relationship. Great companies, great armies, great churches, great sports teams, and great homes all have one thing in common: They have learned to communicate effectively with one another. Communication is not talking. It is listening, observing, studying, and, finally, talking. People who only learn to talk are not communicating; they are spewing. To open up good communication lines with your parents, there are 3 things you must always tell them.

1. Tell them when you need help.

It may be in school, a relationship, or a job, but if you need help and guidance, let your parents know. That's why God gave them to you—to help you get through tough times.

2. *Tell them when you've made a mistake.*

It might be easier at the time to try to cover it up, but honesty not only will help you avoid this same mistake in the future; it will also earn you big points in the "trust quest."

 ### 3. *Tell them you love and appreciate them.*

Sure, there's no such thing as a perfect parent, but most have made a very significant investment of time, energy, and money in their children. Regularly let your parents know you love them, even if they don't always show the same love in return.

liberal in giving

gen-er-ous

characterized by a noble or forbearing spirit[vii]

You're never too young to be generous. It always means so much to me when my sons are generous with a cheerful heart. I just want to do a little jig. That's the kind of giving your parents notice. It makes us so grateful—so very grateful!

You're not too young to give at home. Give to your brothers and sisters. I'm not talking about money or gifts. I'm talking about just acknowledging them, being thoughtful to listen to them. You may have different interests, so just take a little time to listen to their hopes and dreams. Pray for them. Be kind to their friends. All these things go a long way.

Another place where you're not too young to give is in church. Find out where you can serve. Maybe you can help in the nursery. Maybe you can sing.

You might be one of those greeting types. Giving of your time is so generous.

I also want to talk to you about tithing. I learned about tithing when I was about 14 years old. I need to tell you, once you start to tithe, if you haven't already, you're in for the gift that keeps on giving.

Malachi 3:10 NIV says, "'Bring the whole tithe into the storehouse, that there may be food in my house. Test me in this,' says the Lord Almighty, 'and see if I will not open the floodgates of heaven and pour out so much blessing that you will not have room enough for it.'"

The tithe is 10 percent of your income, and it's important to understand that part of being God's daughter is being obedient to His Word. You might think it sounds a little crazy, but God even says to *test*, or *prove*, Him in this.

All I can say is *just do it*, and watch how He will give you wisdom with the rest of your money. He'll even give you ideas on how to make money. It's wonderful to know that you are trusting God with something you've worked hard for, that you've given something you put your heart into. Now, that's giving. Commit to do this. You'll be blessed, and you'll be a part of blessing your church.

Being a generous friend is something God expects you to be, too. Be the kind of friend that you want your friends to be to you. Sometimes a good way to decide how to help your friends is to put yourself in their shoes. What would it be like to be in their circumstances? Just ask the Lord to give you ideas and wisdom.

God wants you to give more than you even want to, because when you're generous with your time, your money, your gifts, and your talents, people see the love of God that's been shed abroad in your heart by the Holy Spirit—and that's exactly what it's there for: to give!

think pink

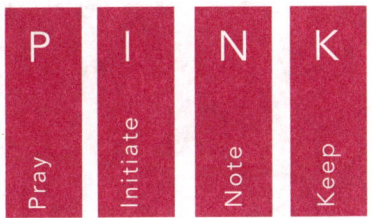

P - Pray
I - Initiate
N - Note
K - Keep

Just out of the blue, ask your mom, dad, brother, or sister if there is anything you can do for them. Even better, just do something for them that you know will help them out. Surprise them. What a way to show God's love!

gen-er-ous

pink ponder

All the flowers of tomorrow are in the seeds that we sow today!

—Unknown Author

pink power

3 ways helping your parents helps you

"What do I get out of this?"

I'm glad you asked. Perhaps you get an allowance that you can point to as some form of payment for your help with the family chores. But maybe not. We've never had a regular allowance with any of our teenagers, but they've always worked very willingly because they care about our family and understand that rewards will come. So here are 3 ways helping out Mom and Dad will help you even more.

Welcome to training camp for life's big leagues.

I'm so glad now that my parents instilled great work habits in me when I was a teenager. They gave me all that I would need to make my bosses happy and get me many raises along the way.

You are sowing seed that you will harvest in your own home one day.

I believe one of the reasons my 3 boys have always been good workers in our home is that I was a good worker in my house. The Bible says that God is never mocked and that any time a seed of any kind is sown, you will reap in due season. (Gal. 6:7.)

 Helping Mom and Dad gives you favor with them.

It won't be long until you really need something from your parents. Every willing, well-done work puts another good deposit in your favor account with them. Withdrawals are easier when you've put something in the bank.

hon·or

one's word given as a guarantee of performance; integrity

one whose worth brings respect or fame

Ephesians 6:1 NIV says, "Children (daughters), obey your parents in the Lord, for this is right. Honor your father and mother"—which is the first commandment with a promise—"that it may go well with you and that you may enjoy long life on the earth."

I'm sure some of you can quote this Scripture backwards, forwards, and inside out. But if not, it's never too late to put this one in your heart. It really goes without saying how important it is for us, as God's daughters and daughters to our parents, to obey this. It is one of the Ten Commandments, so that says something.

The Lord wouldn't ask us to do this if it weren't going to benefit us, just as the Scripture says. God promises us that if we obey and honor our parents, it will go well with us and we'll enjoy a long life on the earth. He also wouldn't ask us to do this if it weren't possible.

Notice that the Scripture says, "Obey your parents *in the Lord.*" You are not required to obey any parent or authority figure who tells you to do something that goes against the Word of God. Most parents are trying their best. Both my husband and I grew up with parents who didn't know the Lord. If you're in the same situation, then you have a perfect opportunity to show the love of God. Honoring them is the best way.

If you don't have Christian parents, please know that even the strongest of Christian families have struggles. As a mom of three great and good boys, I've messed up so many times. I thank God for His mercy and for the forgiveness and understanding of my kids. Please tell me you'll forgive your parents, and don't ever give up on them! Speak well of them, pray for them, and show them respect.

Offer the same honor to the other authority figures in your life as well, such as grandparents, pastors, teachers, and coaches. Tell these people you appreciate them.

Tell your dad and mom you love them. I don't think you can ever tell your family you love them too much. Your family might not be really affectionate, but you can get the ball rolling. Pass out some hugs once in a while.

Show your dad and mom you love them by helping out. Whatever God has asked you to do, He has without a doubt given you the ability to do it. He wouldn't ask us to obey our parents if He didn't think we were capable. Ask the Lord to help you. Ask Him to show you His heart towards your dad and mom. Shock them. Go for it. Clean that room. Empty that dishwasher. Go the extra mile! It's the little things that will bless their socks off, and you'll feel pretty good about yourself too. And the Lord will say, "That's My daughter!"

We need to do our best to be Christ-like at home. Your dad, mom, brothers, sisters—and pets, too—need to know that God loves them. The Bible says that as Jesus is, so are we to this world. His love and kindness flow through us.

It's been said that who you are at home is the real you! That's a thought. Let the Lord help you be His ambassador in your home by honoring your parents. You can do all things through Christ who gives you strength!

think pink

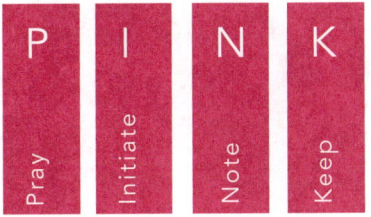

COLOSSIANS 3:20 AMP

Children, obey your parents in everything, for this is pleasing to the Lord.

hon-or

pink ponder

> Be not ashamed of thy virtues; honor's a good brooch to wear in a man's hat at all times.
>
> —Ben Jonson[ix]

7 things a parent loves in a teenager

The Bible tells us that a wise child will make her father happy, but a foolish child will cause her mother grief. (Prov. 10:1.) The attitudes and actions you display in your home can have a major influence on the happiness of your family.

Here are 7 things you can do to bring joy in your family.

 Do your chores without someone asking you to do them.

 Offer to help with something around the house that is not usually your responsibility.

 Think of a compliment you can give your mom or dad, or both.

4. Ask your parents if there is anything you can do to improve your behavior.

 5. When asked to do something, don't procrastinate even a minute. Go right to it.

 6. If you have a brother or sister, treat your sibling with the same respect that you would want in return.

 7. Be polite, thoughtful, and helpful outside of your home: at school, at church, and in other activities.

thank-ful

expressive of thanks
well pleased: glad

The Bible says, "Every time I think of you, I give thanks to my God" (Phil. 1:3 NLT). Even though I might not know you, I truly am thankful for you. As I prepared to write these devotions, I prayed for all the young women who would read this book. In prayer, I have thanked God for you, that you are growing closer to your heavenly Father every day, and that this book will help you.

I, myself, don't have any daughters. I have 3 wonderful sons. Some of my dearest friends have daughters, whom I just love, and I also have 3 precious nieces who are very sweet and a lot of fun to be around.

I am thankful for all of the women whom God has blessed my life with. I am so thankful for moms, daughters, sisters, grandmas, aunts, cousins, nieces, and girlfriends. Without all of us, God wouldn't have His daughters, and we wouldn't have each other. The world just wouldn't be the same without us. God bless His girls!

As we talk about thankfulness, let me ask you a question.

Would you rather hang around people who are thankful or unthankful?

Take a moment to think about the times you have been around ungrateful, complaining people. It's not very much fun. What's really bad is if you're one of them!

Have you ever stopped and listened to yourself? You can't possibly get away from you. But you can take a good look at your heart and mind, and you can ask the Lord to help you change your attitude.

I think we've all been guilty of being unthankful from time to time. I've caught myself several times, just by myself, grumbling to myself. It's so not beautiful. That's why the Word of God says to not worry about anything but instead make our requests known to God. He also says to give thanks in everything. That doesn't mean to thank God for everything bad. It means that even in unpleasant circumstances, we can still have a thankful heart because our trust is in a good Father!

Make up your mind to be a thankful person. Settle it once and for all. It just has to be done. Not only will you like being around yourself, but others will also want to be around you.

This is a good time to bring up manners. Appreciation is so much a part of being a godly young woman. Saying "thank you" to people means so much. You know, don't you, how nice it is to receive a thank-you note? It means a lot to just be gracious and say "thank you" to your server or the little gal at the mall who helped you. You might be that little gal who works at the mall or restaurant. Oh, how your feet ache and you just want to go home! It means a lot to you to hear someone say, "Thank you so much. Have a nice day."

Being God's daughters isn't about being self-centered or just about what God and everyone else can do for us. Instead, let's think about what God can do through us for others. I guarantee you that with that attitude, you won't be able to help but be a very thankful, grateful young woman.

Let's do it. Let's be the most thankful girls in town!

I wish I could meet you and give you a big hug and say, "Thank you for reaching out to others with a heart full of thanks!"

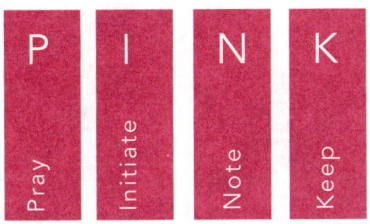

PHILIPPIANS

4:6 NIV

Do not be anxious about anything, but in everything, by prayer and petition, with thanksgiving, present your requests to God.

thank-ful

pink ponder

A thankful heart is not only the greatest virtue, but also the parent of all other virtues.

—Cicero[xi]

3 reasons your relationship with your parents will affect your career

Your relationship with your parents is simply preparation for the rest of your life experiences, including work and career. There are at least 3 important reasons why your career will either succeed or fail as a direct result of how you get along with the authority in your house.

If you can't honor and obey those who love you in your home, it's unlikely that you'll behave any better with a boss who won't be nearly as likely to forgive.

Remember: Your parents will be the last bosses you have who can't fire you.

Your parents have already been where you are headed.

They have experienced the real world. If you're smart, you'll ask questions, listen to their experiences and wisdom, and learn what it takes to succeed.

There will be times when school, chores, and life at home will seem boring and redundant.

The day will come when you will experience the same feelings with your job and career. Learning to persevere and rejuvenate your passion will put you ahead of the pack.

to inspire with courage, spirit, or hope

to spur on: stimulate[xii]

Being an encourager is a very important job God has given us. We can learn everything we need to know about encouraging others by looking at Him. The Bible says our Father is an encourager:

> All praise to the God and Father of our Master, Jesus the Messiah! Father of all mercy! God of all healing counsel! He comes alongside us when we go through hard times, and before you know it, he brings us alongside someone else who is going through hard times so that we can be there for that person just as God was there for us.
>
> *2 Corinthians 1:3,4 MSG*

I hope and pray that you've known what it's like to be encouraged. I pray that as you read these devotions you know more than ever how great you are and how precious you are to God. We all need to hear that!

Some people are just naturally very comfortable at encouraging others, while some have to work a little harder at it. Let me take just a moment to encourage you right now that you can do it! You can cheer people on.

The Bible says, "A word aptly spoken is like apples of gold in settings of silver" (Prov. 25:11 NIV). Another version of this Scripture says, "The right word at the right time is like a custom-made piece of jewelry" (MSG). Take your pick: gold apples or lovely jewelry. Both sound good to me!

Just remember: The Lord is counting on us to speak good, kind, uplifting, helpful, comforting words to people; words that bring hope and faith. Our words can change someone's life.

God's Word also says, "Words kill, words give life; they're either poison or fruit—you choose" (Prov. 18:21 MSG).

Besides speaking kind words, there are other ways to encourage people.

Words can be put on a little note. I have received notes that I've read over and over. It might have taken that person 2 minutes to write it, but it will help me for a lifetime.

A smile goes a long, long way.

A compliment does too!

A little gift lets a person know you're thinking of them and that you and God love them and care! (It doesn't have to be expensive. Maybe it could be a little candle or a tiny picture frame.)

Tell someone you'll pray for them. Now, remember: You mean business. If you say you're going to pray, then pray! A good idea, if possible, is to pray for them right then and there!

Make a phone call. As you're going through your day, a person may come to mind not just once but several times. Sometimes you need to stop and pray for them. Often you could just give them a quick phone call and say, "I've just been thinking about you. Is there anything I can do for you?"

A quick little e-mail can encourage someone too. The e-mails I send have to be quick because my typing isn't that great. "Short and sweet" is a good e-mail motto.

These are all ways that our Father can use us to encourage others.

Now, how can you get encouraged?

Well, I believe God will speak to others to encourage you, but the very best way is to try to remember to go to Him first. He's your Father. He knows you better than you know yourself and knows exactly what you need. He can encourage you like no one else. I love the saying "Go to the throne (God's throne) before you go to the phone."

As God's daughter, you are privileged to enter into His throne room. When you're discouraged, it takes faith to enter His gates with thanksgiving and His courts with praise. You might not feel like it, and that's why I say it takes faith. Get your Bible out, and read some psalms out loud. Faith comes from hearing the Word of God. Sometimes we just gotta do it!

When you're discouraged, that's the time to run to your heavenly Father. Don't run away. His love and His Word never fail. Hope and faith will begin to rise up in you. Trust in the Lord with all your heart; don't lean on your own understanding. In all your ways acknowledge Him, and He will direct your path. He'll show you steps to take.

We can learn to encourage ourselves in the Lord! Let me tell you, that's a true sign of growing up!

Don't you worry. If you've asked the Lord to help you, help is on its way. Don't limit Him! Nothing can stop His love from getting to you. (Rom. 8:38-40.) He wants His daughter encouraged and equipped and strong so you don't miss out on the wonderful plans He has for you. I'm so excited for you! God bless you, you daughter of the Most High God!

think pink

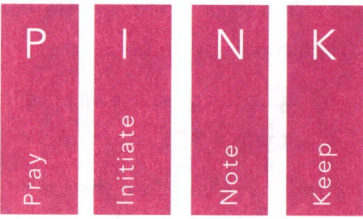

Think about someone you would like to encourage. Write them a note, and let them know what they mean to you. Remind them of how much God loves them and you love them. It only takes a minute, but it can make someone's day— even change their life.

pink ponder

Kind words can be short and easy to speak, but their echoes are truly endless.

—Mother Theresa[xiii]

pink power

encourager

Let no corrupt word proceed out of your mouth, but what is good for necessary edification, that it may impart grace to the hearers.

Ephesians 4:29 NKJV

A little girl came home from a tough day at school and collapsed onto the sofa in her living room. She sighed to herself out loud: "Nobody loves me. The whole world hates me!" Her little brother, who was in the room playing video games, responded, "That's not true, Sis. Some people don't even know you."

He'd had a great opportunity to give some encouraging words to his sister, but instead he'd only added to her frustrations.

If you want people to seek you out as a friend, then be an encourager. It takes a great person to see past people's shortcomings to find the good things and praise them.

re-la-tion-ship

the state of being related or interrelated

kinship[xiv]

In the introduction of this little book we talked about many different hats we wear as God's daughters: daughters to our heavenly Father, daughters to our earthly parents, sisters, granddaughters, nieces, cousins, friends, best friends, students, and the list goes on.

First things first: Our #1 relationship is with our heavenly Father.

One thing God gave us when He made us was a longing to be loved. Did you know there is not one single person in the whole world who can completely fill that longing in your heart? We all do depend on others to fill that longing and hunger in our hearts. But nobody on earth can do it for you: not your family, not your friends, not that prince charming you dream of one day marrying—nope, not even him. And guess what. You will do your best to love your husband and the children God blesses you with, but we all fall short. That's why your first love should be to the Lord. His love never fails, and His love also helps cover our failures.

God first loved us. He chose us to receive His salvation. When we receive that love, we become His daughters. I'll never forget the first time I knew that God loved me.

I was sitting in my room thinking about how many times I had disappointed my dad and mom. I was about 13 or 14 (I wish I had written down the date), and I was with my friends, drinking, smoking, and probably cussing. (It wasn't the first time.) My parents didn't know what I'd been up to, and for some reason (maybe someone was praying) I felt worse than I'd ever felt about myself. I wanted to change so bad but didn't know how. I had been to Sunday school when I was little and sometimes went to church Christmas Eve and Easter Sunday, and I had seen Billy Graham on TV. I was very conscious of God and believed in Him.

I knew there was a Bible on the bookshelf in our family room that my Uncle Freddie and Auntie Ruby had given my dad and mom a couple years prior. I got that precious Bible, sat on my bed, and read Scriptures about God's love until about 4 A.M. There was a section in the front of this Bible that told how to become a born-again Christian. I read and read—and read some more. I cried, and cried some more—first tears of sorrow and then, for an even longer time, tears of joy (real, true joy). I felt so clean and so pure—so forgiven.

From that day forward until this day, no one—not anyone—can ever take away that knowledge of God's love. I knew that I knew that I knew He loved me, and for the first time I had an understanding of what Jesus had done for me. (Rom. 8:15,16.) That night changed my life forever.

Receiving God's love comes by reading and hearing God's Word (His love letters to His daughters) and by prayer (talking to Him and listening to Him). Reading the Word, hearing the Word at church, and praying are things you can do to grow in faith and in the knowledge of God's absolute love for you.

When we make Jesus the Lord of our lives, we are adopted into God's family. He really is our Father. When we are born again, God's Spirit (the Holy Spirit) touches our spirit and tells us who we are and whom we belong to. You are God's daughter. As you gain understanding of that acceptance and love, you will bless others.

Remember: As a daughter, sister, friend, granddaughter, cousin, niece, auntie, wife, mother, grandmother—all you've been called to be in all of your relationships—you will flourish because you, my dear friend, have made the choice to receive the love of God through His Son Jesus. Therefore, you have something so amazing to give: You'll give His best. As God's daughter, you are blessed to be a blessing!

think pink

JOHN 1:12 NIV

Yet to all who received him, to those who believed in his name, he gave the right to become children of God.

re-la-tion-ship

pink ponder

Cherish your human connections: your relationships with friends and family.

—Barbara Bush[xv]

pink power

4 ways to tell parents "thank you"

As you grow in your relationships, I believe one of the greatest character traits that you can develop in your life is appreciation and gratefulness towards others. It's important that you find practical ways to show gratitude to someone who has been a blessing to you. Nothing warms my heart more as a mom than when one of my boys takes the time to tell me and their dad "thanks" for something we've done for them. Here are some ways you can say "thanks."

1. A card.

Take the time to write out your feelings towards your parents, accounting for the specific things they've done that you are grateful for.

2. A gift.

It doesn't have to be expensive. Maybe it's a gift certificate to their favorite restaurant or store. A small sacrifice of finances on your part communicates a big message to Mom and Dad.

re - la - tion - ship

3. *Unexpected work.*

Do something around the house you weren't asked to do: the trash, the dishes, the yard—whatever. Tell them you just wanted to find a way to say thanks.

 4. *Go ahead and tell them.*

Say it out loud, and say it whenever they've done something good for you: a good meal, permission to use the car, a night at the movies—whatever it might be. Tell them, "Thanks!"

a letter from Dad

Dear _____
(your name here)

Before I shaped you in the womb, I knew all about you. I know when you leave and when you get back. You're never out of My sight. I know you inside and out. I know every bone in your body. I know exactly how you were made, bit by bit; how you were sculpted from nothing into something. Like an open book, you grew from conception to birth before Me. All the stages of your life were spread out before Me. The days of your life were all prepared before you'd even lived one day. (Jer. 1:5; Ps. 139:3,15,16.)

I created you in My own image, to reflect My nature. I paid greater attention to you than to any of My creation, down to the last detail—even numbering the hairs on your head! You are My masterpiece. I have created you anew in Christ Jesus, so that you can do the good things I planned for you long ago. I have lavished a Father's love upon you, just because you are My child! I want you to clearly know the plans I have for you. My plan is to prosper you; never to harm you, but to give you hope and a future. (Gen. 1:27; Matt. 10:30; Eph. 2:10; 1 John 3:1; Jer. 29:11.)

Every gift I give you will be good and perfect. I will never change My mind about My desire to help you. If you will simply delight yourself in Me, I will give you the desires and secret petitions of your heart. Call to Me, and I will always answer you. In fact, I'll tell you marvelous and wondrous things that you could never figure out on your own. Remember: I can do anything—far more than you could ever imagine or guess or request in your wildest dreams! I do it by working within you. (James 1:17; Ps. 37:4; Jer. 33:3; Eph. 3:20.)

If your heart is broken, I'll be right there. I'll save you when you are crushed in your spirit. I will care for you like a Shepherd. You are a lamb in My arms, held close to My heart. I'll wipe every tear from your eyes. If you ever doubt My love, remember that I loved you so much that I gave the only Son I had, Jesus, to lay down His life, just so you could live with Me forever. I hope you are absolutely convinced that absolutely nothing—nothing living or dead, angelic or demonic, today or tomorrow, high or low, thinkable or unthinkable—can get between you and My love, because of what Jesus did for you. And one day I look forward to seeing you face to face: tears gone, crying gone, pain gone. Remember that I am coming soon, so keep living by all the words you find in My book. (Ps. 34:18; Isa. 40:11; Rev. 21:4; John 3:16; Rom. 8:38,39; Rev. 21:4,7.)

Love,
Dad...Your Father in Heaven

a daughter's prayer

Father, I come to You, in the name of Jesus, and I thank You for loving me and choosing me to be Your daughter. You gave Your Son Jesus for me. He gave His life so that I can live eternally with You and for You. I know I don't deserve all that You have done for me, so that makes me even more grateful to receive Your love and to know that I belong to You.

I delight myself in You. I trust in You with all of my heart. I don't want to try to figure out everything on my own. I want to hear Your voice in every decision I have to make. I know You will direct me. Thank You for placing Your desires for me in my heart.

Thank You for showing me the right people to follow—people who will teach me and challenge me to be more like Jesus. Help me to be an example to others. I am honored to represent You to this world as I follow Jesus.

I am so thankful that I can come to You with all of my sins and You forgive me. When I lay my head on my pillow at night, I have such peace—a peace only You can give because You've made my heart clean. That makes me want to praise You so much. I know when my feet hit the floor in the morning it's like a new beginning, and because my eyes and heart look to You, I can hold my head high. You give me confidence to take on another day.

Help me to be a giver, Lord. Show me ways to give of myself—my money, my time, and my talents. I want to be Your most generous daughter. You have blessed me to be a blessing.

Let me start right here at home by honoring and obeying my parents. I don't always understand them, and I know they don't always get me, but I trust Your Word. Thank You for Your grace to obey. I know when I give honor and obedience to my parents, it brings honor to You. Thank You for my family, Lord. I don't ever want to take them for granted. Show me ways to be helpful. I choose to speak kind words to my family. One way to bring honor to You and my parents is to be good to my siblings. You have put Your love in my heart so I can be the sister and daughter You have called me to be.

Father, teach me to pray and to worship You in spirit and truth. Spending time with You and hiding Your Word in my heart is what I want to do so my cup runs over to others. They'll know I've been in Your presence. They'll know how thankful I am that You are my Father. I want to be known as a very gracious and thankful young woman. You are so good to me, and I want to tell everyone of Your faithfulness in my life. Use me to encourage people and help them the way You and others have helped me.

More than anything, I desire to grow in the knowledge of You, Father. I want to grow in Your love and Your wisdom. Your Word is a lamp to my feet and a light to my path. As I walk on Your path, help me to be a daughter who pleases You in my relationships with my family and friends and to be a daughter who, above all else, demonstrates Your love and power to those who have yet to call upon the name of Jesus.

Thank You for choosing me to tell others how much You love them and to help You heal their broken hearts. You said in Your Word that the one who wins souls is wise. I don't want anyone to not know the love You've given me. Help me to be a wise daughter leading others to You.

 I *delight* in the Lord.

 I *aspire* to be someone others aspire to be.

 I am *unashamed*.

 I am a *generous* daughter.

 I *honor* my parents and obey them.

 I am *thankful*.

 I *encourage* and am an encourager.

 My *relationships* abound in God's love.

a daughter's prayer

endnotes

i. http://www.m-w.com/dictionary, s.v. "delight."
ii. http://www.wow4u.com/daughters/index.html
iii. http://www.m-w.com/dictionary, s.v. "aspire."
iv. http://www.zaadz.com/quotes/topics/daughters?page=5
v. http://www.m-w.com/dictionary, s.v. "unashamed."
vi. http://www.zaadz.com/quotes
vii. http://www.m-w.com/dictionary, s.v. "generous."
viii. http://www.m-w.com/dictionary, s.v. "honor."
ix. http://www.coolquotes.com/honor.html
x. http://www.m-w.com/dictionary, s.v. "thankful."
xi. http://www.zaadz.com/quotes/topics/thankfulness/?page=2
xii. http://www.m-w.com/dictionary, s.v. "encourage."
xiii. http://www.kindacts.org/quotes.cfm
xiv. http://www.m-w.com/dictionary, s.v. "relationship."
xv. http://www.zaadz.com/quotes/search?page=1&search=Relationships

prayer of salvation

God loves you—no matter who you are, no matter what your past. God loves you so much that He gave His one and only begotten Son for you. The Bible tells us that "...whoever believes in him shall not perish but have eternal life" (John 3:16 NIV). Jesus laid down His life and rose again so that we could spend eternity with Him in heaven and experience His absolute best on earth. If you would like to receive Jesus into your life, say the following prayer out loud and mean it from your heart.

Heavenly Father, I come to You admitting that I am a sinner. Right now, I choose to turn away from sin, and I ask You to cleanse me of all unrighteousness. I believe that Your Son, Jesus, died on the cross to take away my sins. I also believe that He rose again from the dead so that I might be forgiven of my sins and made righteous through faith in Him. I call upon the name of Jesus Christ to be the Savior and Lord of my life. Jesus, I choose to follow You and ask that You fill me with the power of the Holy Spirit. I declare that right now I am a child of God. I am free from sin and full of the righteousness of God. I am saved in Jesus' name. Amen.

If you prayed this prayer to receive Jesus Christ as your Savior for the first time, please contact us on the Web at **www.harrisonhouse.com** to receive a free book.

Or you may write to us at

Harrison House
P.O. Box 35035
Tulsa, Oklahoma 74153

about the author

For more than a quarter of a century, Cathy Bartel has served alongside her husband, Blaine, in what they believe is the hope of the world, the local church. For the better part of two decades, they have served their pastor, Willie George, in building one of America's most respected churches, Church on the Move, in Tulsa, Oklahoma. Most recently, they helped found Oneighty, which has become one of the most emulated youth ministries in the past 10 years, reaching 2,500–3,000 students weekly under their leadership.

While Blaine is known for his communication and leadership skills, Cathy is known for her heart and hospitality. Blaine is quick to recognize her "behind the scenes" gifting to lift and encourage people as one of the great strengths of their ministry together. Her effervescent spirit and contagious smile open the door for her ministry each day, whether she's in the church or at the grocery store.

Cathy is currently helping Blaine raise a new community of believers committed to relevant ministry and evangelism. Northstar Church will open its doors in the growing north Dallas suburb of Frisco, Texas, in the fall of 2006.

Cathy's greatest reward has come in the raising of her 3 boys—Jeremy, 21, Dillon, 19, and Brock, 17. Today, each son is serving Christ with his unique abilities and is deeply involved in Blaine and Cathy's ongoing ministry.

To contact Cathy Bartel
please write to:

Cathy Bartel
Serving America's Future
P.O. Box 691923
Tulsa, Oklahoma 74169
www.blainebartel.com

*Please include your prayer requests
and comments when you write.*

girls about to become

what you think about, you **gab** about, you bring about. you will become what you say.

launch your destiny simply by the things you say. discover how to lay a foundation of success for your future through your words — in love, in school, in relationships, in life. become something great!

Available at fine bookstores everywhere or at **www.harrisonhouse.com**.

Harrison House
ISBN: 1-57794-793-2

find out how you can be a friend to the end...

girlfriends are great!

- wild and crazy,
- quiet and thoughtful,
- fun and exciting.

you can start being a true "girlfriend" to your gal pals:

learn the ropes

get the inside scoop

navigate clichés

stick together

learn to be real

Available at fine bookstores everywhere or at **www.harrisonhouse.com**.

Harrison House
ISBN: 1-57794-794-0

God ideas for a great wardrobe

find out what's hot:

cool clothes

faith

smiles

beauty inside

modesty

God's love

fashion sense. personal style. get them both.

Available at fine bookstores everywhere or at **www.harrisonhouse.com**.

Harrison House
ISBN: 1-57794-795-9

www.harrisonhouse.com
Fast. Easy. Convenient!

- ◆ New Book Information
- ◆ Look Inside the Book
- ◆ Press Releases
- ◆ Bestsellers
- ◆ Free E-News
- ◆ Author Biographies
- ◆ Upcoming Books
- ◆ Share Your Testimony
- ◆ Online Product Availability
- ◆ Product Specials
- ◆ Order Online

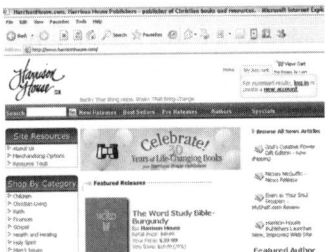

For the latest in book news and author information, please visit us on the Web at www.harrisonhouse.com. Get up-to-date pictures and details on all our powerful and life-changing products. Sign up for our e-mail newsletter, *Friends of the House,* and receive free monthly information on our authors and products including testimonials, author announcements, and more!

Harrison House—
Books That Bring Hope, Books That Bring Change

the harrison house vision

Proclaiming the truth and the power

Of the Gospel of Jesus Christ

With excellence;

Challenging Christians to

Live victoriously,

Grow spiritually.